Editorial Director: Maria Jesús Díaz
Designer: Estelle Talavera
Author: María J. Gómez
Editor: Ana Doblado
Illustrator: F. Valiente / Susaeta
Translated and edited by Lisa Regan

© SUSAETA EDICIONES, S.A. - Obra colectiva
C/ Campezo, 13 - 28022 Madrid
Tel.: 91 3009100 - 91 3009118
www.susaeta.com

English edition first published 2015 by Brown Watson
The Old Mill, 76 Fleckney Road
Kibworth Beauchamp
Leicestershire LE8 0HG

ISBN: 978-0-7097-2230-4

© 2015 Brown Watson, England

Printed in Malaysia

101

FASCINATING FACTS TO KNOW ABOUT

AiRCRAFT

Brown Watson

ENGLAND

Contents

Humans in the sky   6

Flying high!   10

Flying aces   16

Fighter planes   18

Aeroplanes today   24

Large planes   32

To the rescue!   36

High-flying sports   40

Airports   44

Humans in the sky

1 Dreaming of flight

People have always wanted to take to the skies, soaring through the clouds like a bird. It has been our dream for centuries, beginning with setbacks and failures, attempted by a few brave souls who risked their necks – literally – to try to make the dream come true. Many believed it was impossible and laughed at those who thought that one day humans would fly. However, history has shown that the dreamers were right…

2 In mythology

In Greek mythology, Daedalus and his son Icarus were locked in a tower by King Minos. The only way to escape was to fly, so Daedalus made wings out of feathers and wax. Icarus was so excited that he flew higher and higher, until the sun melted the wax and he fell into the sea and drowned.

DID YOU KNOW…?

In the early Middle Ages, merely believing that people could fly was seen as witchcraft.

3 It could have been worse!

Eilmer of Malmesbury was an eleventh century Benedictine monk, nicknamed 'the flying monk'. He believed that the story of Icarus could be made into reality, and built his own wings with a wooden frame. He jumped from a tower at the abbey and glided for around 200 metres. But he could not control his landing, and crashed to earth with a bump, breaking both of his legs so that he could never walk properly again.

4 Leonardo da Vinci

In the fifteenth century this great Italian inventor, inspired by how birds could fly, designed one of the world's first gliders. He also drew plans for the 'aerial screw' which is said to be the forerunner of the modern helicopter. As well as being an inventor, Da Vinci was skilled in painting, anatomy, architecture, botany, science, writing, sculpture, philosophy, engineering, music, poetry and town planning. What a genius!

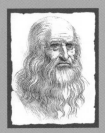

5 The first human flight

…(with no broken bones!) took place in a hot air balloon invented by the Montgolfier brothers in the eighteenth century. Their first trial had no human passengers, but instead carried a sheep, a duck and a rooster! Satisfied with its success, the French brothers then allowed their balloon to carry people on its first untethered journey.

6 A major setback

Jean-François Pilâtre and Pierre Romain were the first people to fly in the Montgolfier balloon. In 1783, they flew over Paris for almost half an hour. However, another flight in a balloon designed by Pilâtre saw them become the first known fatalities in an air crash, when they attempted to fly across the Channel and their balloon deflated and crashed.

7 The arrival of the airship

Airships appeared in 1852. The first prototype was invented by Henri Giffard and he tested it over Paris without anything going wrong, despite strong winds. It had motors and rudders to control its direction and was powered by a steam engine.

8 The glider

A glider is a plane without an engine, which can fly because of the clever way it is is designed. It is steered by moving parts on its wings and tail. George Cayley, a British inventor, built a prototype which took decades to perfect. In 1853 he finally launched a full-size model. No one knows who the pilot was, but he landed safely!

9 The Monoplane

At first, planes had to run down a slope before they could become airborne, or be dragged along at speed to make them take off…until 1874, when French naval officer Félix du Temple's invention, *the Monoplane*, made the first ever successful powered flight.

10 'Sacrifices must be made'

These were the prophetic words of the German inventor Otto Lilienthal, who is considered the father of modern aircraft and was nicknamed 'The Glider King'. He died of injuries after a test flight went wrong.

11 Better and better

Before the accident, Otto Lilienthal and his brother Gustav made more than 2,000 flights to prove beyond doubt that heavier-than-air flight was possible. Their designs took in the brothers' research and findings, and helped to pave the way for the future of aviation.

Flying high!

12 The first planes

The first planes began to be built around the start of the twentieth century. They were heavier-than-air winged craft, powered by one or more engines. They worked on the principals of aerodynamics; air pressure acting on the wings provided the lift needed to keep them in the sky.

13 The Éole

In 1890 Clément Ader was inspired by the flight of bats, leading him to build his aeroplane *Éole*. It had a steam engine, fixed wings, propellors and an enclosed cabin. It managed to fly for 50 metres, but there was no way of steering it!

14 Biplanes

These planes have two groups of fixed wings, usually the same size. They were a huge leap forward in aeroplane stability and manoeuvrability. They have played a key role in military aviation, but these days are seen mostly in aerial acrobatic displays or for use in farming.

DID YOU KNOW...?

The sesquiplane is a variation on the biplane. 'Sesqui' means 'one and a half', and this type of plane has one long wing and one short one.

15 The Wright brothers in the USA

Americans Orville and Wilbur Wright were bicycle makers, but were responsible for many flying firsts. They built the famous biplane Flyer, the first to make a controlled, sustainable flight. In 1905 Flyer III made the first ever nonstop circular trip, and the Wright brothers also made some of the first successful commercial planes.

16 While in Europe...

Alberto Santos Dumont was a Brazilian who moved to Paris, where in 1906 he flew his famous *14-bis* plane for the first time. It was lauded by the European press as the first plane that could really take off by itself. Santos Dumont published all his findings so that aeronautic science could make faster progress.

17 The flying baroness

The French actress Raymonde de Laroche, whose real name was Élise Léontine Deroche, was the first female to gain a pilot's licence, in 1910. Taking part in an airshow that same year, she got caught in turbulence and crashed, leading to such bad injuries it was thought she might not recover – but within two years she was back behind the controls of a plane.

18 Louis Blériot

This French engineer successfully crossed the Channel in 1909 on board his monoplane, Blériot XI. He took off early in the morning from Calais, and landed 36 minutes later in Dover. By doing so, he won a prize of £1,000 offered by the *Daily Mail* newpaper.

19 Why has no one flown across the Atlantic Ocean?

That's exactly what Charles Lindbergh thought, when he set out to become the first pilot to fly solo, nonstop, from New York to Paris. He travelled for over 33 hours in his monoplane, the *Spirit of Saint Louis*, in 1927, making him the first person in history to be in New York one day, and in France the next.

20 Amelia Earhart

She was the first woman to achieve a nonstop solo flight across the Atlantic, and she did so in 1932. The USA aviator spent 15 hours and 18 minutes on board a Lockheed Vega, with only a flask of soup and a can of tomato juice as supplies.

21 Aeroplanes as weapons

During World War I, it became more and more important to be able to use planes. They were seen as a powerful, quick and efficient weapon, but to be used effectively they had to be made faster and lighter, and able to fly at greater heights.

22 Flight assistants

Where would we be without them? But it is a relatively modern profession, as the first airline stewardess, Ellen Church, was hired by Boeing in 1930.

23 Airships

These aircraft manage to fly because they are filled with gas that is lighter than air. They use the same technology as a hot air balloon, although airships are self-propelled and can be steered. The first ones were made of a flexible bag or skin, but bigger, more stable ones used a rigid structure. They are more vulnerable to air currents and storms than an aeroplane.

24 The first Spanish airship

In 1905, Leonardo Torres Quevedo drastically improved airship design. His prototype, called *Hispania*, combined the advantages of rigid airships with the advantages of flexible ones. He sold his designs to the French and British armies.

25 The Zeppelin

Ferdinand von Zeppelin made other improvements to airship designs, and all rigid airships now commonly use his name. His later models had fins and girders and were capable of flights lasting over 12 hours long.

DID YOU KNOW...?

Although airships today are mostly used for advertising or tourism, they were used during World War I for dropping bombs on enemy territory and submarines.

26 The end of the airship

Since 1900, airships have carried more than 30,000 passengers. The *Hindenburg* was the biggest airship the world had seen, measuring 241 metres long and holding over 100 people. Unfortunately, it became even more famous because of the tragedy of 1937, when the ship caught fire and 35 people were killed. Because of this accident, people lost confidence in airships as a mode of transport, and they were no longer used for carrying passengers.

DID YOU KNOW...?

Von Zeppelin founded the first German airline and during World War I it was the first fleet dedicated to carrying passengers.

Flying aces

27 War heroes

According to the French press during World War I, the name 'flying ace' was given to any pilot who had shot down at least five enemy planes. Being a fighter pilot was extremely dangerous, and many were killed, so they were treated as heroes.

28 Adolphe Pégoud

This French aviator became the first 'ace' when he brought down five German planes. Before the outbreak of World War I, he was a flying instructor: he died aged just 26, when his plane was shot by a German pilot who had been one of his pupils.

29 Female aces

The only two female aces were Russians, serving in the Soviet Air Forces during World War II. They were Katya Budanova and Lydia Litvyak. Both of them flew Yakovlev fighter planes and were killed in combat.

DID YOU KNOW...?

Many of the Red Baron's adventures were shared by his faithful dog Moritz, a Great Dane.

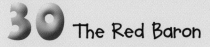 The Red Baron

The German Manfred von Richthofen became a legend by shooting down no less than eighty enemy planes during World War I. His first victories were on board an Albatros D.II biplane, but most of them came on the famous red triplane, the Fokker Dr.I which gave him his nickname.

Fok. F1102.10

Fighter planes

31 Iron birds

During World War I, aviation technology advanced at a dizzying speed. It was the first time that planes had been used in such great numbers. In Germany alone, over 1,200 planes were built!

32 The search for the ultimate plane

At the start of the war, planes were relatively simple and relied on the skills of their pilot. Since then, they have become more important for spying and reconnaissance, and are packed with the most advanced technology.

33 Fighter jets

These military planes are designed for midair combat with other aircraft. To begin with, they were biplanes armed with light weaponry. Gradually they have progressed and are now kitted out with powerful tools for locating targets, as well as weapons.

34 Against all the odds...

Fighter planes vary, from night fighters, adapted for use in the dark or in poor weather conditions with low visibility, to stealth bombers, for air-to-surface attacks that are difficult for the enemy to detect.

35 Firing ace

In 1914 the French aviation pioneer Roland Garros devised a system which allowed machine guns to fire in between the rotating propellors of a plane. In later years, a tennis stadium and the French Open tennis tournament were named in his honour.

36 Jet engines

The jet engine, invented in the years just before World War II, revolutionised the aviation world. It allowed aeroplanes to go faster and higher than any propellor engine could. The German Messerschmitt Me 262 was the first jet-powered fighter plane.

37 King of the skies

The British army's Sopwith Camel shot down more planes during World War I than any other Allied model. It was tricky to fly, but a skilled pilot could get it to perform amazing feats in the sky. It did, unfortunately, spell the end for many inexperienced pilots.

38 Bombers

These planes are equipped with bombs, torpedoes or missiles for attacks on ground and sea targets. This type of mission was originally carried out by airships, but they were not as accurate as the reconnaissance planes which took on the task in later years.

DID YOU KNOW...?

Long range missiles have their own onboard radar to track their target.

39 Boeing B-52

This iconic aircraft is called the Stratofortress and has been in service since the 1950s. It is famous for its long-term involvement in the United States Air Force, and has played an important part in several wars, from Vietnam to the Persian Gulf war, and many operations in countries such as former Yugoslavia, Iraq and Afghanistan.

40 Strike fighters

These planes combine the characteristics of a fighter plane, engaging in air-to-air combat with other planes, as well as carrying missiles and bombs for air-to-surface attacks.

41 Torpedo bombers

Torpedo bombers appeared at the end of World War I, and were used for aerial attacks on ships. They were specially designed to carry heavy torpedoes that were dropped from the sky.

42 Fairey Swordfish

This British biplane was nicknamed 'the stringbag' and helped in the sinking of enemy boats and submarines. It took part in the famous attack on the German ship the *Bismarck*.

21

43 Kamikaze pilots

During World War II, some pilots from the Imperial Army of Japan joined squadrons of suicide bombers to carry out aerial attacks. They flew in planes such as the Mitsubishi A6M, known as Zero, and crashed into enemy targets with the aim of blowing them up and damaging them.

44 Stealth aircraft

These planes are designed to remain undetected by the enemy. They may be made of materials that prevent them showing up on radar and infrared sensors, and their shape is designed to disguise them and make them fly efficiently so they are less easy to hear or see with heat-detectors.

45 Lockheed F-117 Nighthawk

This US stealth fighter was launched in the 1980s. It has taken part in many missions, but it was extremely expensive to run and maintain, so it was retired from service in 2008.

46 B-2 Spirit

This stealth bomber took its first flight in 1989 and is still in service. Its characteristic bird-wing design, curved shape, long range and large capacity for storing and launching bombs, have made it one of the most iconic planes of all time.

47 UAV

This stands for Unmanned Aerial Vehicle – also known as a drone. They are designed to carry out military reconnaissance and attacks, although they also have civilian uses such as firefighting. They have no pilot, but are remote controlled, and can be programmed to take off, fly and land on their own.

48 General Atomics MQ-9 Reaper

This US-based drone was launched in 2001 and is still used today. It has been sent to conflict zones, but has also been important for determining the severity of large fires, and for fighting the drugs war against dealers.

Aeroplanes today

49 Technological advances

In recent years the aviation world has seen many new ideas that make planes safer, both for passengers and for flying crew, and capable of some amazing feats – even taking on more fuel in midair!

50 Cabin pressure

As an aircraft climbs to higher altitudes, the amount of oxygen in the air decreases, leading to breathing problems. The pressurised cabin was invented in the 1930s to make flying more comfortable and safe for the passengers and crew onboard.

Take a peek inside the cockpit! These controls may look like a computer game, but they're for real. They control the whole plane.

NS-236

NS-236

51 In-flight refuelling

Tanker aircraft were invented in the 1950s. These fly alongside other planes and transfer fuel in midair. There are two methods of transfer: flying boom and probe-and-drogue. Refuelling during a flight allows military planes to fly for much longer trips, or to carry more cargo.

52 How probe–and–drogue works

The tanker plane flies in formation with the aircraft that needs to be refuelled. It releases a hose with an enlarged end, which attaches to a probe on the other vehicle. When the fuel has been transferred, the two disengage and both the hose and the probe can be retracted for high speed flight once more.

53 Private jet

These days, some business and several rich individuals own their own aeroplanes. They can be big or small, but usually carry between five and 50 passengers. It is a luxury that only the richest elite can afford – but then, that's what they first said about owning a car!

54 Getting greener

The need for a more environmentally friendly and sustainable way of life means that scientists are trying to improve aviation technology. NASA is also investigating cleaner, more economical energy sources.

55 Solar plane

One of these new advances was Helios, an unmanned craft which consisted of a long wing covered in solar cells which produced the electric needed to power it. It was tested successfully in 2001, but two years later it broke up and crashed into the Pacific Ocean.

56 SpaceShipOne

In 2004 this suborbital spacecraft made its first flight to the edge of space. It was launched in midair by an aeroplane called White Knight and reached 100 km altitude; this was repeated again within a two week period, and the ship and crew returned safely to earth, winning a prize for doing so.

57 Under control

There are several moving sections on an aeroplane that allow the pilot to control it. The ailerons, on the wings, roll the plane to help it turn. The rudders and elevators are on the tail and are for moving up and down as well as turning.

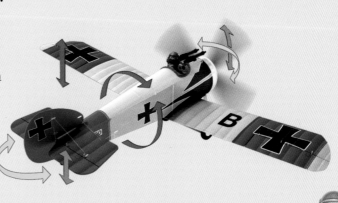

58 Landing gear

A plane has sets of wheels underneath to help it land as smoothly as possible. They may be fixed, and so permanently exposed during flying, or retractable, when they can be withdrawn inside the plane, and operated from the cockpit by the pilot.

59 Fuselage

This is the body of the plane. It is where you will find the cockpit, the cabin where the passengers sit, and the cargo hold. Some planes are narrow-bodied, with a single aisle between rows of seats; others are wide-bodied, with two or more aisles.

DID YOU KNOW...?

The wings are strong enough to hold passengers if they need to escape – that is why the emergency exits are nearby.

 **Wings**

The wings are what really makes flight possible, providing the force that keeps the plane aloft and moving through the air. Nowadays the wings are also where fuel is stored for the flight, and are known as 'wet wings'.

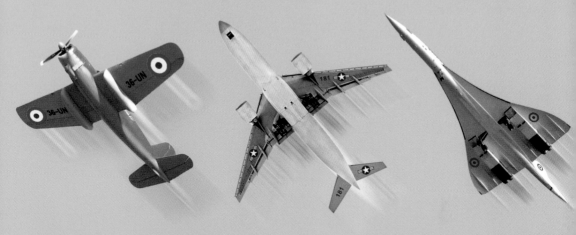

61 Ejector seat

Fighter planes may contain a special seat which allows the pilot to escape in the case of an emergency. The seat is pushed out of the plane at top speed by an explosion, taking the pilot with it. Once they are outside the plane, a parachute opens to carry them safely back down.

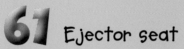

 Autopilot

This facility began to be developed in the early twentieth century, but made even more progress with the advancement of computer technology. Nowadays most procedures, except taxi and takeoff, can be done by autopilot. It can be a great help during bad conditions with poor visibility, and to prevent overtiredness for the flying crew.

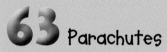 Parachutes

These were first used by pilots in the armed forces during World War I, when the parachutes were made out of silk. It was only after the start of World War II that nylon became available to make parachutes in large quantities, and special fighting regiments were parachuted into enemy territory.

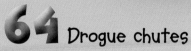 Drogue chutes

Some parachutes are actually attached to the plane: the pilot uses the chute to slow the plane down as it lands, and reduce the amount of stopping space needed. Various fighter planes use this method for extra braking power.

65 The flight recorder or black box

This device records conversations in the cockpit and the plane's flight activity, in case there is an accident. The box is actually orange, to make it easier to find, but is still nicknamed 'black box' because it is usually only needed in tragic circumstances.

66 Supersonic jets

These planes can travel faster than the speed of sound, reaching speeds over 300 m/s. It was once thought that this was impossible but these days nearly all fighter planes are supersonic. There have been two supersonic passenger planes: the Tupolev 144 and Concorde.

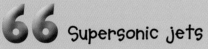

67 Concorde

This is the most famous commercial supersonic plane, and an iconic sight. Mechanical failure in 2000 led to a serious accident which killed 100 passengers, nine flight crew and four people on the ground. The resulting concerns over safety and maintenance costs led to the whole fleet being grounded and taken out of service.

Large planes

68 Commercial aircraft

These planes are used for carrying passengers. After the world wars, airlines concentrated on improving both safety and comfort for their customers. They embrace new technology to make air travel as fast and safe as possible.

69 The aeronautic industry

The invention of the jet engine revolutionised air travel. Nowadays, companies employ highly qualified people to make their air lines as innovative and modern as possible. New prototypes keep the aeronautic industry moving forward in leaps and bounds.

This giant has different floors, 22 landing wheels, and engines which measure 3 metres across. It is one of the most commonly used passenger plane designs.

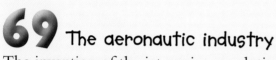

First class

A380

Cockpit

Radar

Bar

Stairs to upper floor

Cargo hold

Restaurant

Landing gear with 22 wheels

70 Airbus A380

This giant plane can carry over 800 passengers and can reach speeds of 900 km/h! The cockpit has eight LCD screens and whole banks of controls. It began flying in 2005 and is the world's largest passenger plane.

Auxiliary power unit

Private cabins

Lift

Kitchens

Rows of seats

Toilets

Rows of seats

Stores

Fuel tanks

Flaps

4 engines, each 3m across

71 William E Boeing

An American pioneer, Boeing dreamed of making air travel available to the masses. He wanted it to be as safe as other modes of transport, but so much faster. He formed The Boeing Company to build aeroplanes, and it became the largest manufacturer of both commercial and military planes.

72 Boeing 747

This plane is also known as the jumbo jet, or 'queen of the skies'. It has four engines and was a forerunner in long-haul passenger flights across the continents. It first flew in 1970 and held the record for the most passenger capacity until the Airbus A380 came along.

73 Havilland DH 106 Comet

This was the world's first production commercial passenger liner, and began flying in the middle of the twentieth century. It suffered several design problems which caused accidents, and various models were released, but it was eventually taken out of service at the end of the century.

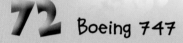

74 F-16 Fighting Falcon

This is a multirole combat plane, first used by the US Air Force in the 1970s. It is no longer used by the US military, but is exported around the world. Over 4,500 have been produced, and sold to over 20 countries.

DID YOU KNOW...?

The Airbus A380 uses more than 800 km of cables, weighs over 550 tonnes, and has 15 escape slides to evacuate passengers if there is an emergency.

75 Harrier

The Harrier is an amazing aeroplane that does not need a runway, as it can take off and land vertically. It began military operations in the late 1960s and is still in use today.

To the rescue!

76 Not just for travel

Humans are always thinking of new ideas and machines. Simply inventing something is never enough; it can always be changed and improved. This inquisitiveness has affected the aviation world in different ways. Going faster, being safer, travelling to impenetrable places, saving lives…we have invented planes that can land on water, aircraft that can hover motionless in the air, and even spacecraft that can carry people to the Moon. It seems there are no limits!

77 Taking off on the sea?

Henri Fabre was a French aviator who invented the first seaplane, called Le Canard (which means 'the duck'). In 1910 his plane took off from the surface of a pond, making it the first aircraft to take off from water under its own power.

78 Plus Ultra

This 'flying boat' took off from Spain in 1926 and flew across the Atlantic Ocean, landing in Argentina (Buenos Aires) four days later, stopping in five places along the way. It was the first ever flight between Spain and South America.

79 Amphibious aeroplanes

These planes can not only take off and land on water, but can operate on dry land as well. They have been used in many military missions and nowadays are excellent for fighting fires.

ANFIBIO-BJ-853   NR-231

SEA RESCUE

R-438-NA

80 Boeing 314 Clipper

These luxury flying boats were used briefly in the 1940s for long-range flights across the Atlantic and Pacific Oceans. They carried passengers from the USA to far-flung places such as Singapore, Hong Kong and Hawaii and had a lounge area, dining room with waiters, and beds.

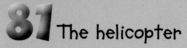

81 The helicopter

Helicopters use rotors to take off, keep them in the air, and move around. They are extremely useful and important for search and rescue, firefighting and surveillance operations.

82 The gyroplane

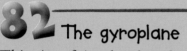

This aircraft is related to the helicopter. It was invented by a Spanish engineer, Juan de la Cierva, who substituted the wings of an aeroplane with a rotor. Its first flight, in Madrid in 1923, was a total success, and five years later it flew across the Channel.

83 Highly manoeuvrable

It was not until 1942 that Ígor Sikorski designed the first fully controllable helicopter. The rotors keep the aircraft aloft but also provide the thrust needed to move it forwards or backwards.

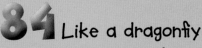 Like a dragonfly

Helicopters are extremely complicated – and expensive – but they are invaluable because they can take off and land vertically, in a very small space. They can also hover in one place, allowing them to carry out tasks that no other type of aircraft can do.

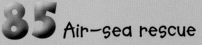 Air—sea rescue

Aircraft are often used to rescue people who are stranded at sea. Skilled emergency crew can airlift people to safety and make sure they receive medical treatment, treating minor injuries and ensuring they don't suffer longterm effects from exposure to the cold and the water. As well as helicopters, hydroplanes are also used, as they can take off and land without a runway. The rescue may be carried out by military units or civilian teams.

86 Mountain rescue

In recent times, professional mountain rescue teams have been able to save many lives. Helicopters allow them to arrive on the scene extremely quickly, and they are able to access even the most remote areas. Searching an area is made possible by the helicopter's ability to hover and fly slowly. These days, the helicopter is equipped with many things needed to give medical care straight away, or to keep the victim safe until they reach hospital.

High-flying sports

87 Adrenaline rush

Improvements in the design of parachutes and flying machines have led to an array of thrilling sports – for anyone without a fear of heights! Enthusiasts take to the skies in gliders, or for the even more daring, there's paragliding and hang gliding, if you're willing to throw yourself into the sky from high places!

88 Hang gliding

This sport uses a triangular wing, or sail, made of fabric. Once airloft, they use air currents to travel over long distances. Some daredevils even perform acrobatics! A World Championships is held about every two years.

Ultralight Gran Sport P2020

89 Competitions

There are several championships around the world, depending on your chosen sport: some are for gliders (with no engine) while others are for aeroplanes and other motorised craft.

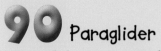

90 Paraglider

A paraglider is rectangular, like other modern sports parachutes, but it is much wider and also more aerodynamic. Pilots can reach speeds of 60 km/h. Paragliding increased in popularity in the later years of the twentieth century.

Ultralight Gran Sport P2020

W-25

91 ASPA aerobatic team

Part of the Spanish Air Force, this team of helicopter pilots perform amazing acrobatics at airshows and exhibitions. They fly in five identical Eurocopter Colibris, a light, single-engine craft with a wide cockpit for better visibility. Each one has a pilot and a co-pilot who are highly skilled and put on an amazing show.

DID YOU KNOW...?

Skydiving is one of the most popular air sports. You jump out of a plane wearing a parachute, which only opens as you approach the ground – just in time to save you from a crash landing!

92 Acrobatics

If you have ever witnessed an airshow, you will know that there are fantastic displays of aerial acrobatics, with planes pirouetting and looping through the air. There are five basic manoeuvres for pilots who wish to enter competitions: lines, loops, rolls, spins and hammerheads (stall turns).

93 Even crazier!

Some air displays contain dangerous stunts – like wing walking! These crazy acrobats are fixed to the top wings with a harness, and perform gravity-defying stunts.

Airports

94 All under control

An airport is a specially designated area for all things to do with air traffic and travel. Outside, you will find everything that's needed for an airline to function, and in the heart of the airport there are the facilities that all the travellers use. Everything needs to work perfectly together in this age of international travel, with millions of people flying around the world each year.

95 Passenger terminal

Passengers arrive and depart from these buildings. It is where they board their plane, book their tickets, or collect their luggage. Terminals these days are like a small town, with restaurants, shops and entertainment areas.

96 Runway

This is the important bit for going up and coming back down! Runways are usually paved with concrete or asphalt, and their position is very important – they do not want a crosswind during this part of the flight. Most aviation accidents happen during takeoff or landing, but fortunately it is extremely rare.

DID YOU KNOW...?

Some airports are in the sea! They are floating on the water, like Kansai Airport, which is built on an artificial island in Japan.

97 Control tower

All of the air traffic is organised from a room at the top of the control tower. The task of the air traffic controllers is hard enough on a normal day, but is made harder when the weather is bad, or the volume of traffic is particularly high.

DID YOU KNOW...?

The airport at Abu Dabi, in the United Arab Emirates, has a control tower that measures 105 metres. It is designed with two giant crescent moons, which is the symbol of the Middle East.

98 Air traffic control

The air traffic controllers are responsible for the safety of all the vehicles in the sky around them. They use advanced computer technology, and equipment such as powerful radar, to allow them to give the correct orders for a pilot who wishes to land or take off at their airport.

99 The luggage conveyor

To make it easier to handle luggage, passengers collect their bags from a conveyor belt that moves automatically. The cases are unloaded from the plane's cargo hold, put onto the conveyor, and gathered up as each passenger recognises their luggage.

100 Security checks

Scanners and X-ray machines check each passenger's belongings to make sure no weapons or other dangerous items are being carried. Airport security also use dogs that have been trained to sniff out explosives or drugs.

101 Heliports

Helicopters may have their own airport, called a heliport, which is much smaller and simpler than one for aeroplanes. They can be surface-based (built on flat land), raised (situated at the top of a building) or platform (installed offshore or on ships).

Index

A

Acrobatics   10, 40, 42, 43
Ader, Clément   10
Aerial screw   7
Aeronautics   11, 32
Airbus A380   32-35
Airport terminal   44
Airship   8, 14, 15, 20
Airshow   12, 42, 43
Air traffic control   46
Amphibious plane   37

B

B-2 Spirit   23
B-52   20
Biplane   10, 11, 17, 18, 20
Black box   31
Blériot, Louis   12
Boeing 747   34
Boeing, William E   34
Bombers   20-23

C

Cabin pressure   24
Cargo hold   28, 32
Cayley, George   8
Channel   8, 12, 38
Cierva, Juan de la   38
Cockpit   28, 32, 33
Commercial plane   31-34
Control tower   46
Concorde   31

D

Da Vinci, Leonardo   7
De Laroche, Raymonde   12
Drone   23

E

Earhart, Amelia   13
Ejector seat   29
Éole   10

F

F-16 Fighting Falcon   35
Fabre, Henri   36
Fairey Swordfish   21
Fighter plane   16, 18-23, 30, 35
Firefighting   23, 37, 38
Flight assistants   13
Fuselage   28

G

Garros, Roland   19
Giffard, Henri   8
Glider   7-9, 40
Gyroplane   38

H

Hang gliding   40
Harrier   35
Havilland DH106 Comet   34
Helicopter   7, 38, 39, 42, 47
Helios   27
Heliport   47
Hindenburg   15
Hot air balloon   8, 14

I, J, K

Icarus   6
Jet engine 19, 32
Kamikaze pilots   22

L

Landing gear   28, 32
Lindbergh, Charles   12
Lilienthal, Otto   9

M

Malmesbury, Eilmer of   7
Messerschmitt Me 262   19
Montgolfier brothers   8
Monoplane, The   9
Monoplane   12

N

NASA   27

P

Parachutes   29, 30, 40-42
Paraglider   40, 41
Pégoud, Adolphe   16
Pilâtre, Jean-François   8
Plus Ultra   36
Propellors   10, 19

R

Radar   20, 22, 32, 46
Red Baron   16, 17
Rescue   36, 38, 39
Richthofen, Manfred von   17
Romain, Pierre   8
Runway   45

S

Santos Dumont, Alberto   11
Seaplane   36, 37, 39
Solar plane   27
Sopwith Camel   20
SpaceShipOne   27
Spirit of Saint Louis   12
Spying   18
Stealth plane   19-23
Supersonic   31

T, U

Tanker plane   25, 26
Temple, Félix du   9
Torpedo bomber   21
Triplane   17

V, W, Z

Wings   6-8, 10, 23, 27-29, 38, 43
Wright brothers   11
Zepelin   14
Zeppelin, Ferdinand von   14, 15